COTTAGES

First published in Great Britain in 1991
by John Hine Limited, 2 Hillside Road, Eggars Hill,
Aldershot, Hampshire GU11 3NB
This edition published in 1991

Picture credits:
National Trust, Wessex. Page 8
Collections/Brian Shuel, London. Pages 18/19
Syndication International Ltd, London. Page 21
National Trust Photographic Library/Mike Williams, London. Page 29
National Trust Photographic Library/Fay Godwin, London.
Pages 31 and 32

ISBN 1 871754 05 4 Stone Cutters Cottage & Purbeck Marblers Stone Cutters

Printed by Centurion Press Limited, London.

FEBRUARY

STONECUTTERS COTTAGE & PURBECK MARBLERS AND STONE CUTTERS

BY

JOHN HINE

Contents

2

INTRODUCTION

3

PURBECK MARBLERS AND STONE CUTTERS

27

STONE CUTTERS COTTAGE

37

THE GREAT, GREAT, GREAT, GREAT,
GRANDSON OF A SMUGGLER

68

DAVID WINTER

72

AND FINALLY.....

Introduction

From the most famous Scottish tradition of Burns night, we next take a look at the least famous (and now almost defunct) English one. I very much doubt that anybody outside the Isle of Purbeck has ever heard of it, but we included it in the series because it is all about stone, which is a material much in evidence in David's cottages and because it demonstrates a problem that continually cropped up - how to keep the family together through local employment, something not always easy to achieve.

David has created in Stone Cutters Cottage a friendly home in which one can imagine how much the parents wanted it to be the centre of their childrens lives.

The Purbeck Marblers and Stone Cutters

You and I have at least two things in common; we collect David Winter Cottages and we are descendants of the caveman. These bonds should bring us close together.

Today, we are masters of our planet and have nothing to fear in our environment. Millions of years ago, the caveman could not say that, as he was a meagre creature surrounded by terrifying beasts that could gobble him as we would a peanut. He lived in what really was a hostile world and he needed a safe home for his family. The cave provided just such a secure retreat. No tyrannosaurus rex could threaten him once he was deep inside his cave. His children could play freely and life could be sweet, albeit somewhat claustrophobic. When the caveman needed more space, he hacked out the stone with primitive tools and piled the unwanted rocks outside the cave. A few million years went by before anybody had the bright idea of piling the rocks on top of each other to form a wall, subsequently a house. So stone became man's favoured building material. Its advantages were enormous as it was free and in abundance; it lasted forever, it didn't burn, it came in whatever size one wanted and any structure built in stone could be made into a fortress.

This last point was most important as man has spent most of his time on this planet killing his

Top: No tyrannosaurus could threaten him. **Above:** Early man's primitive tools

Above: *Stone alone protects*

neighbours, either the next door tribe or the adjoining country. This manic preoccupation with war has meant that nobody was safe unless they were behind stout stone walls that could be defended against the latest gang who wanted what did not belong to them and would happily take it unless deterred. Stone was the best means of doing that. 'Stone alone protects'; as the slick copy writer of ancient times might have written. Much of the history of long gone civilisations is gleaned from the ruins of towns and cities, which thankfully were built in stone and easily revealed by the archaeologist's trowel. Houses made in wood are lost forever and we know very little about them.

Stone comes in all colours, textures and grades of hardness. While some are so soft they crumble like a crispy bread roll, others are so tough they are almost impossible to cut and have to be hacked out of a cliff face with pickaxes. Eventually, dynamite made these unmalleable types easier to

Left: *A young apprentice hard at work*

handle. Some stone is comparatively soft when cut in the quarry but becomes much harder when exposed to the elements, which makes it the easiest and best to use.

Many of David Winter's cottages depict stone features, either foundations for timber framed buildings or the whole building being of stone. He has to know the local texture and building traditions to make the piece authentic or his mail-box will bulge with letters pointing out that the detail was incorrect. Collectors like their artist to get these things right, as indeed he should. This involves David in a great deal of research and observation but he enjoys it as it makes his task more interesting and demanding. He has to make a different miniature tool for each type of rock he sculpts; making the tool inevitably takes longer than applying the detail to his original wax. As his blind collectors have told him, they can feel the stonework and can see in their minds what shape it is in and the type of texture.

Stone has dominated every aspect of architecture for thousands of years and is a fundamental part of David Winter Cottages, so we were delighted when we came across a little known British tradition that we could include in this collection. It is called 'The Annual Meeting of the Ancient Order of Purbeck Marblers and Stone Cutters', not one of the most famous traditions, I grant you, in fact none of us had ever heard of it until we started digging in to the archives when researching the whole subject of British Traditions. The activities at today's "meeting" are a relic of earlier times when apprentices were initiated into their guild.

The guilds started in medieval times and were a sort of trade union, that attempted, and usually succeeded, in maintaining a closed shop for itself. With the stone cutters, this was done by limiting the number of apprentices to the amount of work that could be foreseen. In hard times, no apprentices were allowed in so that what little work there was could be shared out amongst those already employed. In prosperous times, there was avid competition for the best and brightest young men to be signed up.

For a clever lad with his wits about him, this presented a considerable opportunity to be made a

Above: *A bright lad might be wined and dined*

fuss of by the guild masters, all of them proffering inducements to join their trade and telling pernicious stories about the dangers of joining the other guilds.

One such youngster almost made a living out of being "head hunted" in those prosperous days in the seventeenth century when Britain was going through a positive boom. His name was Herbert Bracethwaite and he was as sharp as a butcher's blade. He was intelligent, strong and by all accounts, had the making of being a first-class tradesman. One after the other, the guilds sought him out and invited him to supper at the Inn where they plied him with sack and ale and fed him on beef and mutton. The plasterers, the cobblers, the vintners, the taverners and the stonecutters all hosted him, until Herbert started believing that he must be rather special, with all this attention being paid to him. Little by little, he began to put on airs and graces and soon became a larkspur, a cocky young upstart. Needless to say, the Guild masters

Above: *Receiving membership of the Guild*

found this hard to put up with, but they had to recruit good apprentices if their trade was to flourish. With more work to do than good men to do it, they were desperate. So they humoured Master Bracethwaite and tolerated his considerable lack of modesty and ever increasingly insufferable ego. The weavers, the spinners, the coopers and haberdashers all made overtures and extolled the virtues of their particular guild. Herbert had never had it so good! Awash with beer and stuffed with victuals, flattered abominably and pampered outrageously, our Herbert became intolerable. He strutted and swaggered around the town like a young buck in full prime. Now, it is a curious feature of homo sapiens that we all love to see the vain and conceited get their come-uppance and the more Herbert lorded it over all and sundry, the more his nearest and dearest longed for the day he'd get his just desserts.

They did not have to wait long, as the guild masters tired of their pursuit of uncatchable quarry and decided amongst themselves to punish the arrogant Herbert Bracethwaite as he thoroughly deserved. One of the guild masters invited him to be his guest at supper in the local hostelry, where, unbeknown to Herbert, all the other guild masters would be waiting for him. As he walked through the door, they all pounced on him and stripped his clothes off him down to his essential undergarment.

Above: *As he walked through the door, they pounced on him*

Above: *Rolling the barrel*

They then painted thick, black, sticky tar all over him and bundled him into a barrel filled with feathers. They then rolled the barrel down the street and pulled the prostrate Herbert out and strapped him into the ducking-stool. The guild masters took it in turns to dunk the now wretched lad into the foul and stinking cow pond. Word spread around the town that some goodly sport was to be had at Herbert's expense and soon all his family and friends arrived to witness the humiliation of Herbert. He would have endured anything but the indignity of having this happen to him in front of everybody he knew. Oh, how the mighty were fallen. Without a scrap of his former good opinion of himself left intact, he skulked away into the dark back alleys, there to bemoan his devastated state of mind and paltry condition of dress.

Nobody knows how he repaired his tarred and feathered body or what happened to him next as he disappeared from the town, without saying a word to anyone, perhaps not surprisingly. Twenty years went by with not a word of his doings or whereabouts. He then turned up out of the blue and set up a workshop as a whitesmith, making and repairing agricultural and trade metal implements and tools. He took on apprentices and trained them in his skills. When the boys finished six years apprenticeship, he insisted that they were ceremoniously certified as craftsmen and made to go

Above: *The Annual Meeting of the Ancient Order of Purbeck Mar*

and Stone Cutters

through the unpleasant business of being tarred and feathered. This tradition remains intact hundreds of years later and is still the custom in some parts of the English Midlands today. Herbert Bracethwaite's revenge was perpetrated on tens of thousands of youngsters over three centuries. So who had the last laugh is rather difficult to decide.

The Annual Meeting of the Ancient Order of Purbeck Marblers and Stone Cutters is the ceremony of inducting apprentices into the stone industry. The purpose of the meeting is to decide how many apprentices should be allowed to join the Guild. Too many brought into the ranks would be putting existing jobs in jeopardy, by having insufficient work to justify the enlarged workforce. On the other hand, if times were prosperous and the order book full, they had to ensure there were enough craftsmen to do all the work or contracts would be lost to other quarries. The meeting had to weigh up the economic outlook and future prospects, against

***Above:** Corfe is a small village*

the potential number of apprentices in the pool who could be recruited.

In times gone by, these were sometimes hard decisions to take, because the elders would often be talking about the future of their own sons. Corfe Castle is only a village and regular jobs were not always easy to find. Coming from a quarryman's family, the boys would expect to follow in their father's footsteps and would be unlikely to find a position in either of the alternative industries of farming or fishing, because sons of these harvesters would be favoured before 'outsiders'. Should the Guild decide not to promote all the available apprentices, then a major problem would have to be faced by the unlucky candidates and their families. The options were limited, the lad could go to Portsmouth and try to enlist in the Navy or venture even further to the sea-faring city of Bristol and work his passage to the Colonies - there to take pot-luck with whatever he could find to do. Undoubtedly, the son would be lost from the bosom of the family and much crying would be witnessed on the day of his departure, for the chances of ever seeing him again were remote. The elders knew that keeping the closed shop too tight could well cost them their own sons, but to be too liberal could lose them their own employment and put them in the same predicament as their offspring, but without the benefit of youth being on their side. One can easily imagine the tension inside that little room in the town hall of Corfe Castle, when it seemed as if there was no chance of taking on all the young men, thus virtually signing a deportation order for some of them to leave their family and village and seek their fortunes elsewhere.

The actual ceremony is rather curious, but these young men are more fortunate than the whitesmiths (or engineers as they are now known) as the worst that happens to them is having to pass down a passageway formed by established craftsmen and attempt to get from one end of it to the other without spilling a single drop of beer from their tankards which are filled to the brim. The older men push, jostle and trip the apprentices and generally do everything they can to make the lads spill their beer. Sounds a silly way of spending a fine afternoon, but that's what they do and a jolly good time is had by one and all. This lark is preceded by a procession from the Fox Inn down

Above: *The craziest game of football*

the village street to the Meeting Room where the master craftsmen meet to discuss how many new apprentices to recruit. Not too many men are invited to the Annual Meeting as the room is tiny and can only accommodate about 10 small to medium sized craftsmen and that is with them all holding their breath and stomachs in. I have seen records which show that this Annual Meeting was described as 'ancient' in the year 1611, so heaven only knows for how many centuries this tradition has been going on .

After the meeting comes the fun and games with spilling, or rather not spilling the beer. Then they all go off and play the craziest game of football that I have ever heard of. The background to this part of the tradition is all to do with establishing a right of way over the fields that separate the stone quarry from the small port from where the cut stone would be shipped to London or wherever. The quarriers don't own the fields and would be land-locked if they were prevented from taking their wagons across them, so they re-establish their right-of-passage by kicking an old leather ball along the track, once a year. You would have thought this is all unnecessary as the stone nowadays is taken by a walloping great truck along the main road and there isn't the slightest chance of needing to take a team of horses with stout carts laden with stone across the bumpy fields, but that is missing the whole point. The British love their ancient traditions and will go on perpetuating them until Armageddon, for no other reason than that it has always been done that way. The time will never come when that tattered old ball isn't being kicked, perish the thought. I am sure that our friends in the New World must think we have all had a touch too much sun or something, because we cling to the time honoured old ways and demonstrate a rigid determination to hang on to them at all costs - this is what British Traditions are all about.

Stone Cutters Cottage

David rarely strays from his concept of a house being a family home and the place where family life is led. This is apparent in Stonecutters Cottage and we could not find it difficult to imagine the close knit bond between parents and children in this warm and cosy building, that is as solid and purposeful as the Dorset family who would have resided inside it.

Dorset is one of my favourite counties, because it is all on a small scale, with hundreds of quiet villages and plenty of countryside between them. The county has never been industrialised and has kept its roots firmly planted in agriculture and rural activities, so there is much clean air to breathe and enough beauty in buildings and landscape to keep anybody happy for a hundred lifetimes. The people are solid, like their Purbeck stone, and reliable, worthy and straightforward. What matters to them is the quality of their lives, measured in terms of those long held principles and honest values, which gives

Above: *Dorset, with quiet villages and countryside in between*

them peace of mind and that feeling of cleanness which comes only by sticking to challenging standards and setting stiff examples for the children to emulate. This does not make them stuffy and unsmiling, far from it, they are not riddled with problems, so happy, cheerful faces with big outgoing smiles are the norm.

Thomas Hardy, the great English novelist, poet and dramatist, who lived between 1840 and 1928, was born in Dorchester, which is 16 miles, as the crow flies, from Corfe Castle. His father was a stonemason, who would have spent his entire life sawing, carving and laying Purbeck stone. Hardy wrote many fascinating novels, set in his beloved Dorset, with broodingly descriptive passages that brought to life the undercurrents of human relationships.

Some of his books have been made into films, which enable us to feel how it was to live in the

Above: *Thomas Hardy's cottage*

Left: *The grandiose beauty of Corfe Castle's imposing ruins*

days he wrote about, and bring the passions and frustrations of life sharply into focus. "Far from the Madding Crowd", "The Mayor of Casterbridge" and "Tess" ("Tess of the D'Urbervilles") are some examples of the film maker's art, bringing to life the work of a great writer. His novels are full of real characters, with strong emotions, who are absorbingly interesting and hold one spellbound throughout the long books. Hardy exposes every thought and aspect of his chosen subjects and breathes life into them, until one is convinced they really lived. His Dorset farmer or grandiose beauty are never dull, but are always different and deeper than one could believe.

These county characteristics and the stone from the Purbeck quarries, were David's starting point, when, in 1989, he was thinking about his Stone Cutters Cottage. He wanted it to reflect the enduring qualities of the people and their insistence on holding onto their time honoured ways, in this part of England where so much (progress) has been kept away. They have not succumbed to the glitzy dazzle of some of the world's new ways, nor been tempted to throw away their forebear's beliefs, and try out a way of living that is shallower and less demanding. This cottage stands on the soundest foundations - this thought is uppermost in the mind as one looks at it and senses the solid and firm construction. No short cuts have been made here

and the builder has kept to his traditional methods and materials. The hearth at the bottom of the main chimney is central to the building and would become the focal point of life within it. Here the family would gather after their hard day's work, the men from the quarry, blasting and cutting the stone, the women from gathering wood, tending the cottage animals and crops, and taking part in the harvest, depending on the time of year. The assembled adults and children would warm themselves in winter and enjoy a wholesome stew, with most of the ingredients from their own garden. And so to bed in the tiny bedrooms, with windows no bigger than they had to be, to prevent that bone chilling wind, that blows down the coast from the Arctic, from keeping the family warm and able to comfortably sleep the night through, in their solid and well heated little Stonecutters cottage.

The Great, Great, Great, Great, Grandson of a Smuggler

Not far from Corfe Castle, but still in the county of Dorset, is the small country town of Beaminster, which is a veritable haunt of Hines.

In the eighteenth century, the place was full of them, as the old parish registers record. Even today, the surname is to be found in abundance and one cannot move in any direction without bumping into a Hine. Butchers, bakers, candlestick makers, all

The popular business of smuggling

have borne the name, but there was one particular member of the family who in 1740 went into what at the time was a popular business - smuggling.

Since the Romans left these islands in AD 490, the English do not seem to have been able to brew a decent alcoholic beverage other than ale and cider, while the Scots have become pre-eminent in the distilling of Whiskey. Dorset is about 400 miles

A cider press

A ship could travel fast with a fair wind

away from the distilleries of Scotland and only 60 miles, by sea, from France. A sailing ship, given a fair wind, could travel faster than a horse-drawn cart being driven over pot-holed tracks, so France was infinitely more accessible than the land of Robert Burns. The British have always had a penchant for good quality liquor and there has always been a good market for enterprising men of commerce, who could deliver the finest wines and spirits to the

The King levied a heavy tax

City of London and its prosperous surroundings. Unfortunately, this trade was hampered by King George the Second's insistence that a heavy tax must be levied on these imports and he built up the number of Excise Men, who had the task of collecting the duty and passing it on to the King, so that he could finance his grand plans of enlarging the infant British Empire and consolidating his influence over the American and Canadian colonies.

He was fairly successful at this, a great deal more so than his inept grandson, George the Third, who allowed a gang of Bostonians to upset the grand scheme by chucking best quality tea into their harbour. Not only did we, the British, lose the tea and never got paid for it, we also never did collect the tax and lost the colony to boot. George the Second would have prevented such a scandal, and would have been more subtle and cunning, and kept his cotton and tobacco growing territories firmly within his control. Never mind - it is no good crying over spilt tea!

In those times, one would be taking a most considerable risk if one attempted to bypass the official channels and bring into England casks of brandy, port, claret and madeira without stumping up the King's share. He would hang, draw and quarter such offenders to discourage others from having a go and demonstrating what happened to those who defied the law. However the King did

The cunning George II

It was impossible to sell spirits at the proper price

not impose a moderate tax which was not worth going to a lot of trouble and expense to avoid paying, instead he set a huge tariff of customs dues that gave birth to the whole smuggling industry. Indeed, it was impossible to sell spirits at the proper price, as there was so much contraband about at only a fraction of the price of the legalised liquor. This inspired enterprising entrepreneurs all along the south coast, to buy sailing vessels and to take their

Buying a fast boat

chances with the Excise Men. One such was a lad by the name of Thomas Hine, who lived in the town of Beaminster, pronounced Bemster. He bought himself a fast boat and hired a crew of desperados. They set sail for France, rounded the coast of Britanny and continued down the west coast until they came to Rochefort, where they no doubt ate the delicious ewes milk cheese. Here they sailed inland for 75 miles along the Charente river, until they arrived at the town of Cognac.

Presumably he failed to find here the quality of brandy he was looking for, knowing how discerning his customers would be, because he finally weighed anchor 10 miles further inland at the smaller town of Jarnac. I do not know how he came to meet the brandy maker Philippe Conto, but one imagines him searching for the very best and accepting nothing but a brandy that was smooth, fulsome in flavour and delicate on the palate. One can only surmise that he deemed Philippe's the most outstanding and

N
W
E
S
Map of
Thomas' Journey
to
France
LONDON
Southampton
Paris
Jarnac
Limoges
Bordeaux

Searching for the very best brandy

He also met Cecile

of a quality worth risking his life for, when returning to Dorset. He also met Philippe's daughter, Cecile, for whom he developed strong feelings of affection.

Thomas bought a cargo load of brandy from Philippe, with funds raised from only the Lord knows where (I expect a monied Dorset landowner, who would require a cut of the cargo and total anonymity). Thomas returned to the English

Thomas bought brandy with funds from unknown sources

On a moonless night, he made the crossing

He hid his prize securely

Channel and waited for a moonless, misty, night on which to make the hazardous crossing and safely land his prize.

He hid it away securely, while he made arrangements for the barrels to be taken to the city inside carts laden with timber, farm produce or even stone. No doubt, he sold the brandy most successfully, as he returned to Jarnac many, many times and on each occasion got to know Cecile a little better.

This could have gone on for years and developed into an idyllic money-making project, with Thomas retiring at an early age with a handsome fortune. However, the seed of his downfall must have been sewn at this time by either a disgruntled crew member, or one of his conspirators in Dorset, because, on one fateful evening, the Excise Men laid an ambush for Thomas at the point on the coast where he made his landing. The Excise Men relied almost exclusively on paid informers, and because there was so much money to be gained for the King by stamping out the smuggling industry, they were able to be generous with their bribes. Someone tipped them off, because they not only knew the exact location of the landing, but also the expected time. The Excise Men were heavily armed and so were Thomas and his men. As always, it was pitch-black on the fateful night when Thomas brought his

There was much money to be gained from turning smugglers over to the Excise men

They brought the casks ashore by rowing boat

ship to the beach and starting bringing the casks ashore in the rowing boat. The King's men waited until all the barrels and all the crew were ashore and then struck. Shots were exchanged, but it must have been difficult to see a target. Soon swords were drawn and a great deal of close combat was to be he hard. Thomas saw that he was hopelessly outnumbered and called to his men to flee. Some ran off into the scrub beyond the beach, some took

Left on the beach was a body

their chances in the sea, but Thomas and a few of his crew were able to get back to the boat, hoist sail and disappear into the gloom of the misty night. Left behind on the beach was a body, that of a dead Excise Man - Thomas was now a hunted man, being both a smuggler and a man at whose door would be left the consequences of killing one of the King's men. We do not know whose musket-shot killed the Excise Man and for all I know, it could be what

WANTED

THOMAS HINE
FOR
MURDER
SMUGGLING
AND GENERALLY
OUTRAGIOUS
BEHAVIOUR
REWARD £5000
(AND THE GRANGE)
DEAD OR ALIVE

Thomas returned to France and laid low

is called nowadays "friendly fire", but as leader, Thomas would be hounded for the rest of his life and, if caught, would pay a dreadful price for the dark deeds of that black night. Thomas returned to the French coast and laid low until the news of the full extent of his predicament reached him, through gossip in the taverns, where sailors drank and swapped stories. On learning of his predicament he resolved to return to Jarnac and stay there for the

He and his crew set sail for the last time

rest of his life. He and his crew set sail for the last time to Jarnac and finally came to rest in their new home. Having been there, I can assure you that this would have been no hardship at all, even without Cecile to pass the time of day with. Thomas and the surviving members of the battle of the Dorset beach settled down, and set about making themselves useful in the aging Philippe's vinery and learnt the secrets of how to make brandy.

Thomas learnt the art of making brandy

Soon Thomas and Cecile married and had children and eventually Philippe died, and, in his will, he bestowed the business to Thomas.

Wine and Brandy are very often called by the name of the maker and so it was that the brandy Thomas made became known then as Hine Brandy, and it is still known as that to this day. I have no connection with the Hine Brandy business, which may be just as well, as I don't know whether or not the monarch today is entitled to collect taxes incurred in 1743, but if she is, where does that leave us with the unpaid bill and uncollected taxes due to us in respect of tea delivered to Boston?

What about the unpaid bill?

About David Winter

In many ways, David Winter is like the Dorset folk and the Stone Cutters Cottage, which captures their qualities to a nicety. He is the person most resistant to change that you will ever know. In the twelve years we have been working together, I cannot think of one aspect of him, or his way of life, that is in any way different from the way it was in 1979. When not "on parade", he wears the selfsame slip-on shoes, crumpled threadbare jeans and moth-eaten old sweater, that he has always worn. Every Tuesday evening, we sit in the same chairs in the same pub, drinking the same brew and talking about the same old things and it is wonderful.

Almost everything else in my life changes, because of the dictates of business, but my one point of sane constancy is The Professor, who is a staunch pillar of stability and is as solid as a rock of Purbeck stone. Change is foreign to him and he abhors it, as if it were a threat, somehow demonstrating that he believes he will lose something precious through being unfaithful to his set ways and ideals. I was having a go at him the other day about the dreadful state of his cushion covers, which positively glow with being backside polished over years and years. "What's the matter with them", he asked as if they were brand new, "they are comfortable aren't they?" As far as David is concerned, the purpose of a cushion is to soften the hardness of a seat - so long as it achieves that aim, does anything else matter?

Well, you can't argue with that, because it makes excellent good sense. Permanence matters to him, and I thank my lucky stars for that, because without his stable balance and complete reliability, I doubt if I would have remained on the outside of the asylum. The Company has been through twelve turbulent years, with everything moving at breakneck speed, and never a moment to pause to consider what one is doing, let alone why. David placidly stays in his cottage and lets everything pass him by, as he has more sense than to let others navigate the route to his own destiny.

AND FINALLY.....

This book has been mainly about stone and stone-like human qualities. I don't know what Herbert Bracethwaite and my piratical forebear have to do with anything that this book was supposed to be about, but they seemed an entertaining red herring and frankly, subjects I could not resist. The durability of stone gave us stone houses, which had to come before David Winter could sculpt his Stonecutters Cottage for us. The whole book is intertwined with the cord of stability, not only with the stone for building, but the attitudes of the Dorset people, which are so remarkably shared by David Winter and the amazing points of similarity between his life and that of the stonecutter from yesteryear.